MY SAFE Word IS Poetry

JAI THOOLEN

A Picklepoetry Book

picklepoetry@outlook.com

Copyright © Jai Thoolen

No part of this publication may be reproduced in any form without the written consent of the author.

ISBN 978-0-6482030-9-4

Printed by Ingramspark via Lightning Source

For more from Picklepoetry go to:

www.facebook.com/picklepoetry

www.instagram.com/picklepoetry

www.picklepoetry.com

First printed in 2018.

1. *Introduction* 7
2. English Language 8
3. Stories 10
4. Writer's Block 11
5. Ideas 12
6. Acatalectic 13
7. Time 13
8. Books 14
9. Impedimental Thpeech 15
10. Average 16
11. Speed of Life 17
12. Lost Words 18
13. Ode to the Sun 19
14. Mine was Purple 20
15. An Army 21
16. Buttercup 22
17. My Pen 23
18. Mine Reaches the Floor 24
19. My Fingers 24
20. That One Guy 25
21. The Building Site 26
22. Beard 28
23. Life 30
24. Grandpa 31
25. A Boy's Imagination 32
26. Drunken Scotsman 33
27. The Hand of Men 34
28. The Hand of Men Again 35
29. Alchemist 36
30. The Future Never Gets Here 37
31. My Masterpiece 38
32. Freak 42
33. Macca 43
34. Fuckin' Macca 47
35. A Hero 48
36. As Good as Henry Lawson 49

37. I Am	50
38. The Grass is Greener	51
39. You are Special	52
40. Colours	52
41. Moments	52
42. Counting the Stars	53
43. Poe-TRY	54
44. No Magic	55
45. Zugzwang	56
46. Perhaps the Moon	58
47. The Night	59
48. I Can Time Travel	60
49. Will Fate Pick Me?	62
50. Skeletons	63
51. My Monsters	63
52. Bones and Skin	63
53. Kalend	64
54. God's Rant	65
55. Does the Sky?	68
56. My Only Friend	69
57. Ink and Quill	70
58. Lady Spring	70
59. A.M and P.M	71
60. Dear Diary	72
61. Be You	74
62. Ice Age	75
63. Twice	76
64. Poison	77
65. What if I Never?	78
66. If a Tree Should Fall	79
67. Perfect Murder	80
68. A Message	82
69. Dead Man's Moon	83
70. My Friends	84
71. Promises	85

72. My Demons *86*
73. The Old Asylum *87*
74. Grace the Stars *88*
75. Why? *89*
76. Albert *90*
77. The Full Moon at Midnight *92*
78. Footprints *93*
79. Follow *94*
80. Dancing Warmth *96*

A big thank you William, Judith, Michael, Ariane and most of all Sarah.

Introduction

 Hello there. I hope you enjoy this diverse selection of works and words that I've compiled. It's scary to share thoughts and feelings but here we are. I enjoyed writing each piece and I hope you enjoy them too. Don't take me *too* seriously. I'm a tongue-in-cheek sort of guy with a twist of literal and lateral.

Thank you for reading. It means the world to me.

Your favourite author, Jai.

English Language

So, what is all this bother,
Between a comma, and, Oxford, comma?
Periods are called full stops and you'll see them more than once.
Semicolons are peculiar ones;
Apostrophes aren't always fun.
Ellipses are used often and always in a bunch...

Question marks should not offend.
Do they always go where questions end?
Capital letters are for names or where a sentence starts.
Exclamation marks for emphasis!
Sometimes use parentheses,
To separate extra info (or keep some words apart).

Hyphens make one word from two,
In examples like the 'air-crew'.
Talking marks are for saying things, like, "How are things with you?"
Adjectives are to explain,
What is different, what is plain.
Nouns and verbs are words to name the things you see and do.

English seems to never end.
Split infinitives to mend.
Nobody should not use double negatives these days.
An hour, *a* university.
Our language, its diversity.
It tries to Freudian slip us up each gold along the way.

Grammar and punctuation,
Explain the situation.
A book I had had had had the pages all torn out.
It was the entire section,
That taught of preposition.
There are several grammatical rules that sometimes cause us doubt.

Then the silent letters,
Are *not* making things better.
A knight might knock in autumn for rendezvous with Colonel Tongue. So, listen to your teacher.
English is a quirky creature.
Writing will be easier if all the traps have been pre-sprung!

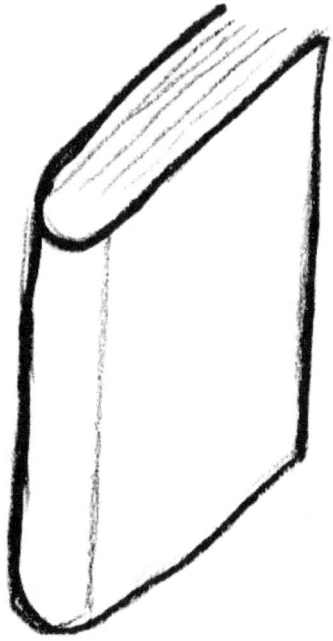

Stories

Punctuation and letters arranged on a page.

Explaining the story and setting the stage.

Five hundred pages of story in print.

Lead to an ending with only a hint.

Chapter to chapter telling the tale.

A heroine to triumph or hero to fail.

Ups and downs are read every line.

Mostly the ending will all turn out fine.*

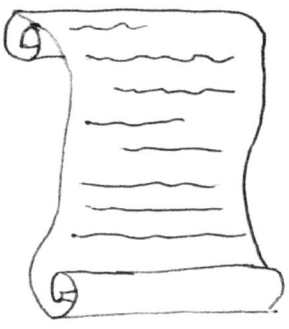

There are trials and tests all along the way.

Using only words to describe and convey.

There are feelings and heartbreak and lovers who've lost.

There are villains and heroes who are double-crossed.

There are adventures to have in faraway lands.

There are treasures buried beneath the sands.

All in this manuscript, scribbled and penned.

An idea, a beginning, a middle, an end.

Mostly.

Writer's Block

Writer's block must be a myth.
The "old wives' tale" kind.
'Cause I've not come across it yet.
The words leap to my mind.

I could be cursed with "writer's free"?
I'm guessing that's a thing.
My pen could be enchanted with,
The ghost of R. Kipling?

I do not know why I can't stop,
Putting pen to paper.
I only know I don't believe
All this writer's block caper.

Writer's block must not be real,
Or wouldn't it get me?
I'll just keep writing rhymes and verse,
I guess we'll wait and see…

Ideas

Each idea I've ever had,

Writing rhymes and more,

I find it's all been done,

A thousand times before!

But instead of giving up,

I write it all-the-same,

Because no one writes it my way,

Or signs it with my name!

Acatalectic

I'm naught if not eclectic.

So diverse in what I write.

I keep acatalectic.

Rhyme and metre to delight.

I know some find it harder.

But I like to challenge me.

I set about with ardour.

To create my poetry.

Time

Time will last forever!

Though, all of us will not.

With no one there to measure,

Would time, in essence, stop?

Books

Books are disappearing,
As the Internet rolls on.
I'd hate to see it happen.
I'd hate to see books gone.
They've shaped the way I deal with life.
They've made me who I am.
While the world wide web is mostly all,
Just shams or scams or spam.
I want to see books make it,
To the very final day.
Children hearing stories,
In every different way.
Books will not surrender,
They'll always tell their tales.
We readers are to help them.
We'll fight to tip the scales.
If we want books to make it,
We really can't concede.
Get yourself some books,
And get out there and read!

Impedimental Thpeech

On*th*e upon a time,

*Th*ome word*th* cannot rhyme.

Word*th* like pint and month,

Never rhymed, not on*th*e!

Orange, wolf, and ninth,

Cro*thth*ing all the line*th*.

Mr Holland'*th* Opu*th*

Make*th* thi*th* rhyme ju*th*t hopele*thth*.

*Th*ilver can't rhyme either,

Purple doe*th*n't neither!

It i*th* al*th*o dangerou*th*,

To have thing*th* that endanger u*th*!

Impedimental *th*peech,

I*th* *th*omething they don't teach.

But if you don't *th*uccumb,

It can be overcome!

Average

Just because you're average,
Doesn't make it wrong.
The world needs to have its averages,
That's where you might belong.
But, if everyone was terrible,
And our average wasn't good,
Then you'd need to strive for better,
Just as anybody should.
If we were all not far from perfect,
You'd be average if you could.
Because to be just average,
Would be superbly good.
Well, not compared to average,
In that scenario,
Though humans in their current form,
Have yet so far to go.
Or, your ego could be lying,
Telling you that you're the best.
You could be in bad company,
Where you stand out from the rest.
You could find better companions,
Then find out it's not true.
So don't try living for others,
Try living just for you!

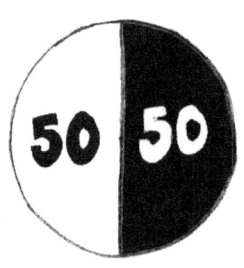

Speed of Life

Age is just a number,
But I'm running out of time.
I'm living at the speed of life,
Already past my prime.

Body no longer agile.
Reflexes slowing down.
I've gained my share of wisdom,
But can't keep hanging around.

To me, it felt like decades.
To time, a single tock.
I'll disappear in history.
Another of the flock.

I'm mostly insignificant,
To all but a close few.
I'm living at the speed of life,
But I'm *living* while I do!

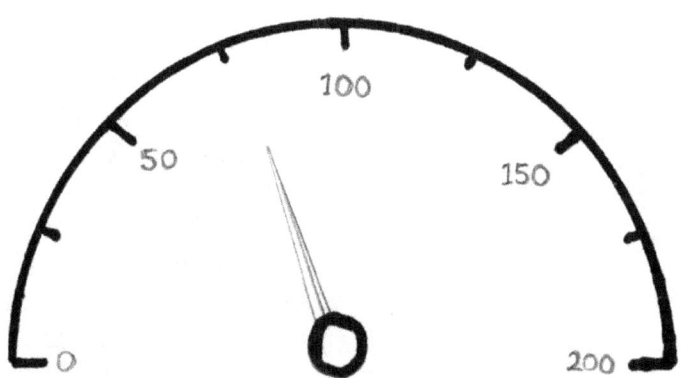

Lost Words

Of all the times,
I've thought of lines,
Just seconds from my sleep.
Perfect sense,
Enlightenment.
They seem so real and deep.

Only to not,
Remember to jot,
Them down for future uses.
So, they remain,
Lost in my brain,
As long forgot recluses.

They shimmer here,
And not quite there,
To tease me of my loss.
So now I wish,
To recall this,
Poetry I've forgot.

The thoughts arrive,
In hurried jive,
As I think I'm winding down.
My head just writes,
A million lines,
And I think "Really? Now?"

I've thought of these things,
My sub-conscious brings,
In quarters, halves and thirds.
Wasted rhymes,
And paradigms.
I call these my 'Lost Words'.

Ode to the Sun (Kinda)

The light you exude often visits,
Even though it takes you eight minutes.
You send it day after day.
Always in much the same way.

With all the practice you've had,
Why are you still so bad?
Of the light that you send I approve,
Though delivery speed should improve.

Eight minutes? You should be at fives…
Second-hand by the time it arrives.
I want all my light to be fresh.
Sun, I don't think you're doing your best!

You've been in this job for too long.
Or somebody showed you it wrong?
I guess you are pretty consistent.
But should bring me my light in an instant!

Mine was Purple

Mine was purple, yours was pink.
Glory, what would mother think?
Such fun we had with each our things.
What fun a good old blowing brings.
Up and down our things would go.
Left and right and to-and-fro.
When I'd finished, mine went down.
So, you wrapped your lips around.
You kindly blew it up again.
Nice and firm and hard and then,
A little friction, yours went pop!
Always too much fun to stop.
But it would all be over soon,
Tremendous joy brings my balloon…

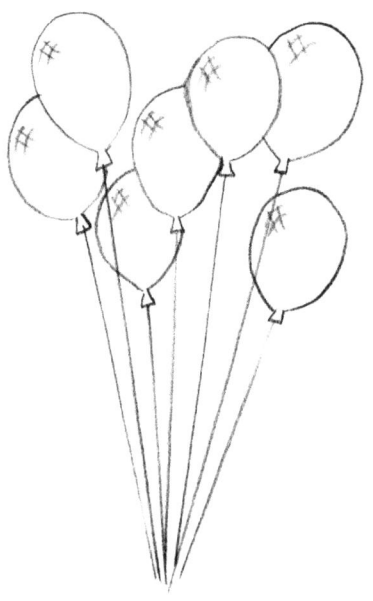

An Army

They marched in as we slept.
The rain covered their tracks.
We noticed them too late.
These troops were maniacs.
They ransacked our supplies.
Everything was lost.
We had to fight them off,
No matter what the cost!
We set a clever trap.
They didn't stand a chance.
We killed them to a man.
Those wretched little ants!

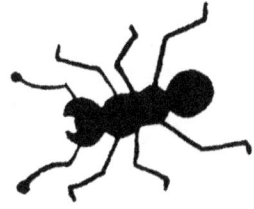

Buttercup

I haven't got a chiselled jaw,
I'm not so broad of chest.
I do not have muscular arms,
But I will try my best.

I shall not shave so often,
I hardly brush my hair.
I fart and burp a bit too much,
But promise I'd be there.

I'm not terribly wealthy,
I stoop and slouch, I know.
I swear a bit and badly,
But please give me a go!

Most women want a man to fix,
Well, *I* could be that him!
A work of art when you are done,
All proper and all prim.

I would dress as a gentleman,
I'd bow when there was need.
If ever there were some debate,
With you I'd have agreed.

I would be deft of vacuum,
Of mop and bucket too.
I'd do all the washing up,
If I could be with you.

Sorry girls, this isn't real.
My pen made all this up!
No such man exists I think.
Unlucky, buttercup!

My Pen

My pen nib is on fire,
It's hot with all the work,
There's smoke trailing behind it,
As my writing goes berserk.
I hope there's no speed camera,
And that it's not a crime,
For pens that speed whilst writing,
For pens, as fast as mine.
As far as pens are known to go,
Mine's easily the best.
I've heard that some folks call it,
'The fastest in the west!'
It writes as fast as Usain runs,
And fast as rockets fly!
It writes the speed of light until,
My pen's ink doth run dry!

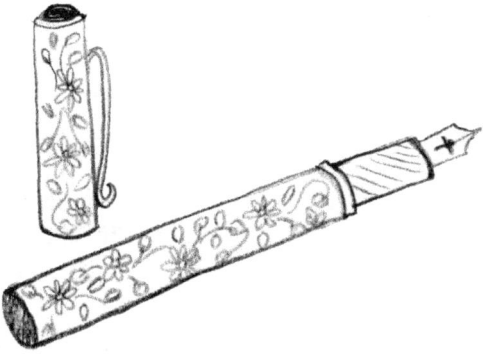

Mine Reaches the Floor

Mine reaches the floor,

It scares them all away.

They never come too close,

They wonder what it weighs.

It hangs there long and proud,

And people think it's weird,

That I move it with a trolley,

My great big, healthy beard!

My Fingers

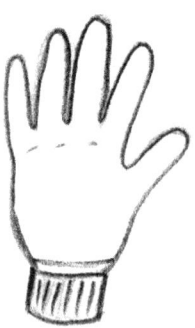

It was a cold dark night.
I knew just what to do.
I put one of my fingers in,
And then another two.
Finally, a fourth,
I gave my thumb a shove.
But I have got another hand,
I'll need a second glove.

That One Guy

There's always one bloke in the bar,
Who cannot hold his drink.
He's in there all the bloody time,
Expert, by now, you'd think.

But he's always fallin' over,
Or talking way too loud.
Gets cut off by 2pm.
His mother must be proud.

He spits on you when talking,
His jokes are never funny.
He never seems to work,
Always try-na "borrow" money.

He smells bad when he's close enough,
He likes to start a blue.
If you don't think this man exists,
I've been describing you!

The Building Site

The brickie's bloody scaffold,
Is in everybody's way.
There's mud all over everything,
He's messing up our day.

The plumber's dug up half the site,
Where we're all trying to work!
The sparky thinks he owns the joint,
The spoilt bloody jerk!

The tiler's put his offcuts,
In the 'timber only' bin.
The grout's not even dry,
They're try-na put the shower in!

The architect's a dickhead,
I think everyone's agreed.
He's drawn impossibilities,
A clue is what he needs!

The builder's bloody hopeless,
He's never even there.
He drops in all too seldom,
He doesn't bloody care.

The concreter built an obstacle course,
That Special Ops can't pass.
There's a battle with the renderer,
Someone'll end up on their ass!

The plasterers have made a mess,
One's in the porta-loo.
The rest are having smoko,
It's all they bloody do!

The chippy lost his pencil,
And he was markin' things in pen.
So the painter had to paint it all,
Again and again and again!

All the little stuff ups too,
The painter has to fix.
Eighteen tubes of 'No-More-Skills'
And other painters' tricks.

Then when the job is finished,
All trades pretend they're friends.
'Cause the next job comes around,
And they'll do it all again!

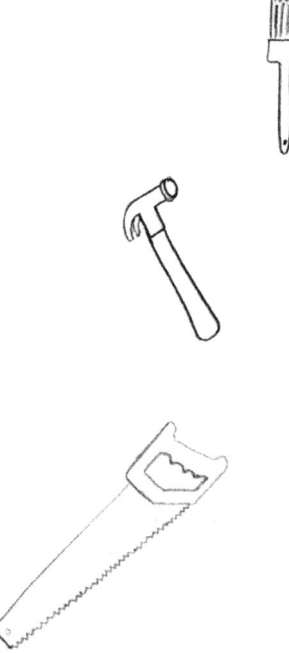

Beard

I like my beard.
You think I am weird.
But I like it more than you know.

I grow it long.
You think that is wrong.
But it will continue to grow.

Encouraging follicles.
A beard that's symbolical.
It keeps my chin nice and warm.

A beard I can brush,
That's bushy and lush.
A beard I can shape and re-form.

My beard is a friend,
When I'm at wit's end.
It makes me feel cosy and safe.

It's comfort to me.
It makes me feel glee.
It won't ever be itchy or chafe.

If only it would,
Grow longer, it should,
Be biggest in all of the land.

But it's only small,
And not big at all.
Not as long as I'd like nor as grand.

I will still try,
And soon maybe I,
Will grow it as long as I need.

People will wish,
For a beard just like this,
A man with his follicles freed.

Life

Please run through the leaves in Autumn,
Dance through the flowers in Spring.
Sing in the rain in the Winter,
And love what the Summer will bring.

Make this a life to be proud of,
Live it loud and full and explore.
Surround yourself only with love,
And always be striving for more.

The life you are living is live,
There isn't a rewind or pause.
Make it more than only survive,
The life you are living is yours.

If you're lucky enough to have freedom,
Do with it the most you can do.
Don't try to be somebody else,
You're the first and the last ever, you!

Grandpa

Grandpa gathers the children.
Oh, the stories Grandpa tells,
Don't seem like simple stories,
They seem like magic spells.

An adventure we're all taking.
New worlds for us to roam.
Mystic paths to travel,
All far away from home.

He takes us on his journey,
In which we are enthralled.
Treasures to uncover,
Magic, jewels and gold!

Legends to discover.
All of Grandpa's thoughts.
Queens and kings and dragons,
Knights and astronauts!

He never tires of telling,
These stories to us all.
He makes us feel like heroes,
Whether we're big or small!

A Boy's Imagination

Each night he went to the land of sleep,
And dreamed his dreams, he dreamed them deep.
One night a pirate, another a knight,
Or flying amongst the stars so bright.

Then during the day, a stick was a sword.
A pot made a helmet, a shield from a board.
A cape from a jacket that was left undone.
A tree was a tower, no end to the fun.

Imagination was all that he'd need.
A princess is captured and needs to be freed.
Keep off the floor! It's lava you know!
Each day an adventure, wherever he'd go.

The car was a monster that he would defeat.
The shed was a gingerbread house he could eat.
The house was a castle that he would defend.
His dad was the villain who'd meet a swift end.

A king or a cop or a fireman too,
He'd stop all the bad guys that he could construe.
He'd win in the end though the battle was hard,
With wizards and witches all over the yard.

The sunlight is poison so stay in the shade!
The garden, an enemy's lands to invade.
His bike was a horse, the fences a wall.
Everything was something or nothing at all.

His cat was a lion, his dog a centaur.
With unicorns and dragons and fairies and more.
This made him happy and brought him such joy.
The wandering mind of an eager young boy…

Drunken Scotsman

Looking across the water.
There is no land in sight.
The ocean's wicked daughter.
Will come for you tonight!

The sea's constant observer.
An evil water sprite.
The waves rise up with fervour,
With passion and delight.

This ship will drift asunder.
A course cannot be set.
The water pulls her under.
Into the cold, dark wet.

No sign but for the flotsam.
This ship will sail no more.
No drinking for the Scotsman.
She will not reach the shore…

The Hand of Men

Once my pen is empty,
Will my writing stay the same?
Is my pen a fair accomplice,
Or the only one to blame?

Do I really play a part,
In anything I write?
Has my pen outsmarted me,
The clever little sprite?

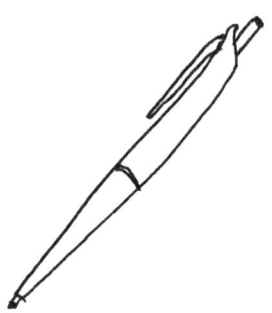

I'll only know once it runs dry,
Who wrote this diatribe.
Was it me all by myself or,
The pen with which I scribe?

If I used a different pen,
Could I write stuff still?
Would I yet be able,
With inkwell and a quill?

Are they all in together,
These pens a scheming lot?
And are the notebooks in it too,
The ones in which I jot?

Do I trust my words at all,
Or would I even dare?
If I turn my back a moment,
Who will plot against me there?

Is my paranoia,
Getting in too deep?
Or will these little bastards,
Try to kill me in my sleep?

Am I over-thinking this,
Should I just calm down?
Are they in control of me,
Each verb I write and noun?

They must be writing this for me,
'Cause I cannot recall,
Getting over sensitive,
Or paranoid at all.

Me, my pen, my pen or me?
Who's written all my work?
Is my pen a mastermind,
And am I my pen's clerk?

Am I like 'The Hand of God",
If only for my pen?
Do I have that backward and,
My pen's the 'Hand of Men'?

The Hand of Men, Again

You know, I think I may have been right,
Because my pen ran dry last night.
I cannot write as I once could.
Things written now aren't half as good.

It matters not how hard I try,
Ever since my pen ran dry.
My writing has not been the same,
And I think my pen is to blame!

For here my pen that wrote it all,
Has no more ink upon its ball.
No longer can it write for me.
Those masterpieces cannot be.

I'll try my best to write again,
Though I'm not sure without that pen.
I cannot write or even think,
Since my poor pen's bereft of ink.

The 'Hand of Men' will be no more!
It's finished up, it is done for.
The pain is real and will not cease.
I cannot write another piece!

Alchemist

I'm a poet of science,

Of alchemical rhyme.

I write pure magic.

I write between time.

I bend quantum physics,

With my pad and my pen.

I exist in dimensions,

That don't allow men.

I can steer sunlight,

And capture the stars.

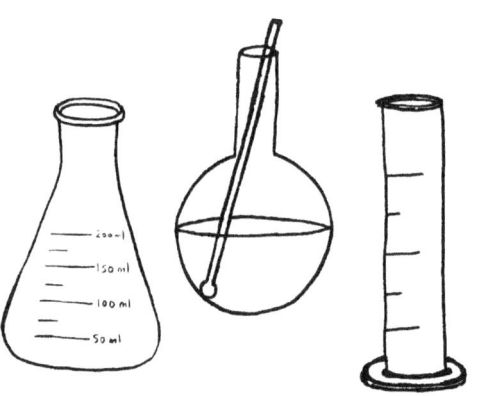

I divided by zero,

And sailed around Mars.

I've drunk molten lava,

Got O.J paroled.

I am an alchemist.

I turn words into gold!

The Future Never Gets Here

I look forward to the future,
But by the time that it arrives,
It has become the present,
And the past never survives.

'Tomorrow' when you get there,
Is 'today' each single time.
'Yesterday' is over now,
Upon the midnight chime.

A today and a tomorrow,
And a yesterday made new.
The new day greets the morning,
The old day bids adieu.

A never ending cycle,
Of destiny and fate.
The human understanding,
Of time and year and date…

My Masterpiece

I sat alone a while,
And thought on what I'd done.
The words had flooded forth.
I knew this was THE ONE!

Though, still I didn't realise,
The scale of it all.
Of what I had just written,
Inside my study walls.

I'd written me a masterpiece!
The likes no one has seen.
A poem for the ages!
By far the best there'd been.

I wrote it in my notepad.
So I would not forget.
There have been some good ones written,
But none were this good yet!

The words became more epic,
As each new line I penned!
I felt the static in the air,
As I scribbled for the end.

My words are on a journey,
They convey amazing tales.
A motorcar on a mountainside,
Just as the braking fails!

My pen and hand were fused as one.
Each word just couldn't miss.
They danced around the pages.
You could surely hear the hiss!

The tides no longer need to turn,
And the sun will never set.
The Earth will even stop its spin.
And old Father Time will sweat!

The Gods all want to see it.
To hear it read or even read,
This epic thing I'd written,
This perfect poetry I bleed!

They'll speak of it forever!
They'll quote it note for note.
This glimpse into my brilliant mind,
This masterpiece I wrote!

Except... nobody will hear it,
It won't be read to one and all!
It won't garner fame or fortune,
Or massive audience, enthrall!

For I misplaced my masterpiece,
And there are no copies or prints!
I put it down on something,
And I haven't seen it since!

I hate that I have lost it,
And that people will miss out.
They'll think I didn't write it,
Their minds will fill with doubt.

At least *I* know it happened.
And I swear these words are true.
I felt all those emotions,
I wish the people felt them too.

The ink it set on paper,
Like a brand upon the skin!
The more I wrote the more it flowed,
The more it drew me in!

It was perfectly amazing!
How could anyone believe,
That I'd written it all by myself,
On a frosty winter's eve?

Folk would wait with bated breath,
To listen to what's said!
On the edges of their seats,
To hear this thing being read!

Some would try to hold back tears!
There'd be others who could not!
A mixture of emotions.
This poem running hot!

Smiling, laughing, longing, crying.
All these feelings opened bare.
All throughout my epic poem,
That I feel compelled to share!

You will hear a mother weeping,
See a man fall to his knees!
It's powerfully dangerous,
When you write poems like these.

It will silence all the Demons,
And make Angels lose their voic
It will start atheists wonderin
And believers will rejoice'

It would have made a difference,
In the lives of many folk.
Made people better people!
If my words were ever spoke!

Our children would await the day,
They'd get to hear it too.
To hear my epic poem,
Begin life again, anew!

I'm so sorry that it's missing.
I've ruined all our lives for good!
If only I'd remember.
I'd rewrite it if I could…

Freak

Roll up! Roll up!
Come see the freak!
It's safe. He is caged.
He is chained and is weak.
This is his life.
Put on show for the crowd.
They jeer and they sneer,
And they gasp out aloud.
He recedes in his cage.
Tries to hide from the throng.
The shame and embarrassment.
The hurt is so wrong.
How such an anomaly,
Defines what they see.
They don't see a man.
How blind can they be?
They don't see a man…
They only see me!

Macca

We'd bowled pretty bad. It looked like we had,
Never played, they made four-twenty-one!
We'd dropped a few sitters and they had some hitters.
We looked to be pretty well done.

But, "We'll give it a crack." I said to the boys,
"You gotta be in it to win it!"
Macca and Bob took the openers' job,
And *their* openin' bowler could swing it.

He could swing it both ways, inward and out.
Bob did anything he could to get on one.
He flicked one down leg that just missed his pegs,
And they scurried through for our first run

It was a worrying time for a little while there,
We were all pretty tense.
It got a bit easier when they bowled him a teaser,
And Mac put it over the fence!

Bob made his way to Eighteen for the day,
Then tickled one through to the 'keeper.
Freddy would fall off his eighth or ninth ball ,
And Terry was out even cheaper!

Mac set his jaw and smashed a few fours,
While Tommy just valued his wicket.
We were going okay, Mac swinging away,
But then, right on drinks, Tommy nicked it!

Four-fa ninety-two from twenty won't do.
Blue and Macca would need to be nifty.
Wherever they'd pitch it, Blue would just hit it,
And he nigh on beat Macca to fifty!

So, I woulda bet now that Macca was set,
They couldn't get him out for tryin'.
He got a few more of those sixes and fours,
And Bluey was still bloody flyin'!

Mac raised his bat and we gave him a clap,
When he brought up his hundred and one.
He'd made it this far, the man was a star,
A real 'Aussie battler', a gun!

Then on ninety-nine it was Bluey's time,
He hit one down deep-square-leg's throat.
Macca still in on one hundred and ten,
And now Mickey to 'steady the boat'.

Mick out for twenty, Mac still on plenty,
I went in for a whack.
Got away with a few, and then ran a two,
And hit one 'bout twenty rows back!

I didn't last long, caught out at long on.
We'd still need a hundred and eight!
Jimmy out quick, try-na smash one for six,
He said "It cut off the pitch and swung late!"

Mac was still in, it was all up to him,
'Cause Dazza and Willow can't get 'em.
They can hold up an end for an over or ten,
But to make runs as well we were dreamin'.

So, Macca went nuts, there were no ifs or buts,
He swung like a mad man possessed.
Five fours in a row, 'bout eighty to go,
To keep strike, the next, he caressed.

He hit fifteen more off the next coupla balls,
Got himself to one-seventy-six.
He needed a breath, he was feeling like death,
And his hands and his arms felt like bricks.

Daz faced a few, it was all he could do,
To give Macca a sec for a breather.
Then Macca went 'smack!' off this poor old attack,
They couldn't believe all this either.

'Leven runs off the next, then twenty-six,
Mac was a freak and he knew it.
We had a real shot, within thirty we'd got,
Nobody had thought we could do it.

Daz blocked some out and got through a few shouts,
But he'd made it through a tough over.
Mac on again and he carved up these men,
With a Six over gully, point and cover!

With just thirteen left, Daz did his best.
He flicked one away for a quick one.
Macca went BOOM! It cleared the clubrooms,
And gave us all hope where we'd had none.

Then Dazza got out when the ball swung about.
There were three balls left for poor Willow.
"Just get through these, mate! Close up your gate.
You could be 'our little hero!'"

Willow got through, he let out a "Phew!"
With a "Good on ya mate!" from Macca.
The very next ball, Mac gave it his all.
The bowler sent down a half tracker.

It was right in the slot and Ohh, what a shot!
Cleared the fence by a bloody mile!
We all ran to him and his big crazy grin,
And carried the man off in style!

The legend lives on, it'll never be gone
How our game that day was a cracker!
They talk of it still and I'm sure always will
Two-forty unbeaten for Macca…

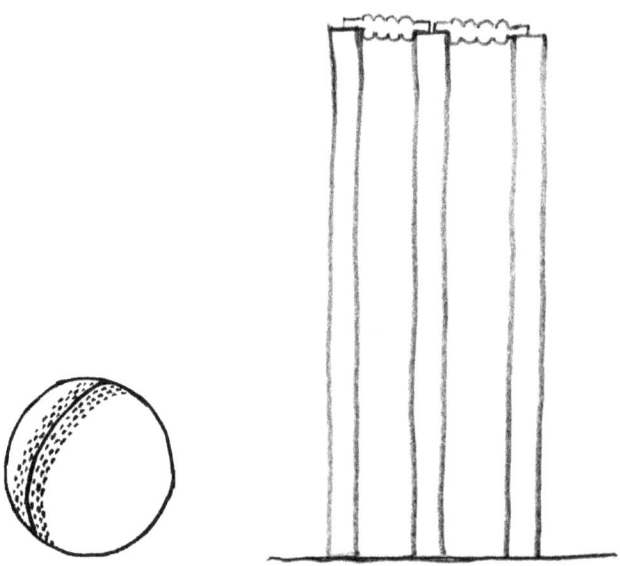

Fuckin' Macca

The day we'd made four twenty-one, we thought we'd done okay.
But nothing had prepared us for what happened next that day.
Beginning slow right at the start, they got up a good clip.
That "Macca" bloke batted bloody well, he really had a dip.

It didn't matter where we bowled, to him, it was more runs.
We got wickets at the other end but not enough t'have won.
Some red-haired guy named "Bluey" tried to hit all the runs at once!
He had a crack and could really whack, he wasn't any dunce!

Ninety-nine he made that time and then we got him out.
But this "Macca" at the other end was *still* smackin' us about!
He wasn't slowin' down at all, he kept hittin' us around.
He trusted in his tail end and they didn't let him down.

They were gettin' "Mac" to get on strike and *he'd* punish us all.
It was like he was a cyborg, the way he tracked that ball.
He peppered sixes everywhere and peppered fours as well.
The bloke was here to fuck our day, as far as we could tell!

And fuck our day he really did as they got past our score.
There was no way on that there day we coulda made much more.
We had batted pretty bloody well. We'd really done our best.
His mates had got not even half… fuckin' Macca… got the rest!

Hero

A busy buzzing worker bee.

All that pollen he collects.

A circumstantial quirk for he.

A queen that he protects.

A hero of his hive,

He'll deliver you a sting.

Although he'll not survive,

He's proud to do his thing.

As he drifts to darkness,

His heart is full and warm.

His duty's done regardless,

A saviour of his swarm!

As Good as Henry Lawson

I've read poems of some famous sorts, Banjo and the like.
I've written some myself at certain stages of my life.
But when I read the words of Henry Lawson it just seems,
The words he writes and uses are the poetry of dreams.

If I could write as he did, happy I would be,
And my poetry world famous and have people know of me.
To share my thoughts and verses with all the people of the Earth.
To know the things of which I write are measures of my worth.

If I could somehow be even half as good as him,
I think I would be happy then instead of glum and grim.
If a solid few like or love the poems I have penned,
That should bring me happiness when I am at my end.

I hope the people like the compositions I create,
And over time I may become quite good or even great!
And should they know my name in north and south and east and west,
To Henry I'd be quite content to be the second best!

As good as Henry Lawson or just fractionally worse,
Every time I put my rhyming prose into a verse.
To write of things I've seen and done or this country that I love,
I wish Henry to be watching me from somewhere up above…

I Am

I am a peaceful individual,
Just trying to get by.
I travel there and here and there,
From place to place I fly.

But some folk are not happy,
When I visit them I feel.
I don't understand their issue.
Even though their issue's real.

The mother tries to rush me.
The father tries his luck.
The children chase me everywhere.
I dive and dodge and duck.

The doorway is my freedom.
If I could only get outside.
There would be so many places,
That I could use to hide.

This life I lead gets tough sometimes.
I'll never quite know why,
They're all trying to swat me!
A friendly, honest fly…

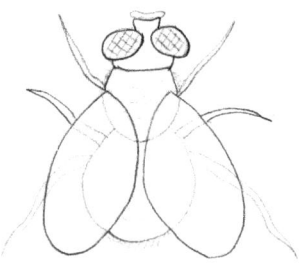

The Grass is Greener

The grass always looks greener,
And it looks nicer and cleaner,
At least from where you've seen 'er,
From your side of the fence!

I know from life's example,
That it seems so lush and ample,
Just another field to trample,
At someone else' expense.

The greener grass you claim,
Turns out to be the same,
Then you need someone to blame,
Who will pay for this offence?

From here *your* field looks greener,
And nicer, lush and cleaner,
The best you've ever seen 'er,
What an odd turn of events!

You Are Special

The stars?
There are many.
You?
Just this one!
Therefore: you're more special, than even the sun!

Colours

If all the world were black and white,
An ashen, greyish hue.
Where would all the colours live?
I think they'd live in you!

Moments

It glistens from the spider's web,
That early morning dew.
These misty days are beautiful,
The warmer ones are too.
There's magic in the colder days,
Each one blessed and new.
Enjoy *all* of your moments,
Each one is just for you…

Counting the Stars

I tried to count the stars one day.
But the sunlight was shining and got in the way.
So, I waited till nightfall and outside I stood,
To count the stars or to see if I could.

I started my count from the west.
I counted the brightest then counted the rest.
There are so many I couldn't keep count.
I couldn't tally a final amount.

I tried the next night and I failed again.
I tried to keep count with my pad and a pen.
The next night I tried with a calculator.
The next night I tried as an estimator.

I tried it for weeks but it didn't go well.
I counted each night but I never could tell,
How many there were a-twinkling up there.
Each night, as I'd count and I'd point and I'd stare.

Never an answer or total I'd get.
I'd keep losing my place or the number, forget.
Because our world spins, centrifugal.
I should put the question to Google!

PoeTRY

I planted me a poe-TREE,
That I water all the time.
I feed it when I get the chance,
Another verse or rhyme.
It grows and grows quite steadily,
I add to it and I,
Would not serve it properly,
If I did not poe-TRY…

No Magic

At the bottom of the garden,
Beneath the ancient elm,
Amongst the moss and mushrooms,
Exists another realm.

One of wondrous magic,
Of fairy dust and spells,
There gnomes and imps and sprites,
And other creatures dwell.

I would go there in my younger days,
And play amidst my friends,
Of elves and trolls and fairies,
Through a child's lens.

Now that I am older,
The fairy folk aren't there.
Imagination's dwindled,
There's no magic, anywhere…

Zugzwang

Fate and Death are playing chess,
You watch every move they make.
You know that it is quite the match,
Then realise what's at stake.

They're playing for your life, you see.
This will decide your end.
Does your life continue on,
Or is your soul condemned?

Will your life be over,
With a clever 'castling' move?
Is it destined to be a long life,
As Death's pieces are removed?

Fate has been a chess player,
Since all of time began.
But Death is also very good,
And has a solid plan.

You cannot look away at all,
You watch the game unfold.
Watching Fate play for your life,
Is *something* to behold.

You're nervous and you're right to be,
As this decides your fate.
Death moves his queen to king's knight four!
Then bellows out, "CHECK-MATE!"

It's over! Your fate is sealed!
How could this possibly be?
Death points to you and beckons.
You plead, "Best out of three?"

Fate turns to you too calmly.
He doesn't need to say.
You read it in his eyes.
It was *meant* to be this way!

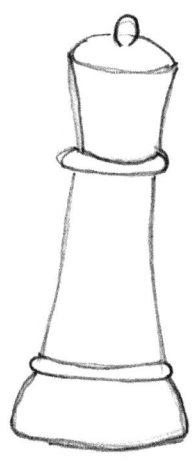

Perhaps the Moon

Perhaps the moon likes deeper water,
And follows where it goes?
They say that's in backwards order,
But who really, truly knows?

Perhaps the moon would like to swim,
But can't get fully in?
She'd like a deeper swimming place,
Where she can wet her skin?

Perhaps the moon needs privacy,
Or a lunar bathing suit?
To conceal away her modesty,
Hide her forbidden fruit?

Perhaps the moon would like to bathe,
And wash away her woes?
Though, without the deeper water,
She can only dip her toes…

The Night

The sun descends behind rolling hills,
And gently slips away.
Shadows grow deep and longer,
At the ending of the day.

Darkness shrouds the subtle shapes,
And stars are silver shining.
Cold and dark surround us all,
The shadows are defining.

Golden rays awake the day,
At early morning hour.
Early birds begin their song,
And brightly blooms the flower.

The hurtling light speeds toward the night,
In repeated daily chores,
And dimming light allows the Night,
To claim again what's hers…

I Can Time Travel

Through the course of my life,
I've come to unravel,
A valuable skill,
That's known as Time Travel.
Not into my past,
Nor to famous dates.
I can't change the future.
I can't alter fates.

The thing I've discovered,
In all of my years,
As each day moves forward,
Our past disappears.
Once it's gone by,
There's no going back.
It's over and done with.
It's faded to black.

I'll get to my future,
Not a moment too late.
As it becomes present,
If only I wait.
Then soon as I get there,
It's NOW and then PAST.
It's done in an instant.
Those moments don't last.

Time hasn't all happened,
There'll be more for some.
The future is coming.
The present has come.
Well, not exactly,
That's not what I meant.
Time keeps on happening,
There's more to be sent.

Okay, there you have it.
The time gone is missed,
But 'cause we record it,
It makes time exist.
I guess what I'm saying,
In these lines of rhyme,
Is I can Time Travel,
At the speed of time…

Will Fate Pick Me?

There are a billion writers,
And many more there'll be.
Words never read, talent forgot,
So, why would Fate pick me?

I'd like my writing published,
And so would many more.
For now my words are hidden,
In my office desk's third drawer.

One day, and if I'm lucky,
Once my book is on the shelf.
I'll sell a million copies,
Of art I made myself.

Do you think that Fate would bother?
Should I make a fervent plea?
Will I ever really make it?
Do you think Fate might pick me?

Skeletons

I have skeletons in my closet,
But please don't misconstrue.
There are none so truly worrying,
And I bet you have some too!

I try hard to not judge others,
Even when I don't agree.
I'm hoping that they feel the same,
And won't be judging me.

My Monsters

When a younger me,
Was what I be,
There were monsters under my bed.
Older, I see,
They've not left me,
They've moved into my head!

Bones and Skin

You are not just bones and flesh and skin,
You're what you choose to be within.

Kalend

January said to

February that

March and

April

May!

June convinced her friend

July to come over and stay.

August started rumours of what

September made her do.

October told

November that

December made her too!

God's Rant

God was sitting at my local bar,
Drinking beer after beer.
All the local barflies stared,
But no one would go near.

So, I sidled up beside old God,
And asked him how he was.
He drew in breath, then turned to me,
Blinked a bit and paused.

*"I'm drowning all my sorrows,
Of which there seem a lot!
I've seen you mortals try it,
So, I'm giving it a shot."*

I offered my best wisdom,
He seemed to take it in.
We disagreed some here and there,
But he took it on the chin.

He told me that his biggest regrets,
Are starving children and wars!
The favourite thing of all he made,
Were all the dinosaurs.

He said, "*Men judge too quickly,*
Of things they cannot know,
And presume to know my feelings,
In all scenarios!"

"*Though, really, they know nothing,*
Of how I feel and think,
And that is why I'm sitting here,
Drowning in my drink!"

"*Men judge those who are innocent,*
Of all but minor sins,
They sin, themselves, too often,
To fly on faultless wings!"

"*I cannot stop world hunger!*
You all, too far, have strayed!
You pray to and you blame me,
But all this is human-made!"

"*All and each religion,*
Have made-up their own rules,
To suit those men in power,
And keep the rest as fools!"

*"I cannot fix all problems,
But I cannot just look on!
I tried to fix this once before,
And gave my only son!"*

*"Know your god is fallible,
You don't need me to live!
But we can work together,
To give all we can give!"*

*"It shouldn't be about money!
You shan't give in to greed!
Shelter, food and loving,
Is all that we each need!"*

*"I'll go now back to Heaven.
Thank you for the beers.
You've helped me here and greatly,
I'll see you later, cheers!"*

I sat alone a while,
And thought on what he said.
Had I been in the bar too long?
Was it all just in my head?

Does the Sky?

We often look up at the sky in wonder.

Does the sky look at us much the same?

We watch the planets and stars that we're under,

The universe from whence we came.

Does the moon or the sun look at us here on Earth?

Try to see how we work, what we're for?

Have the stars wished on us or guessed at our worth,

Or sent one of their own to explore?

Does the sky think we're magic, hold us in esteem?

Do the planets discuss us a lot?

Do the black holes and meteors see us in their dreams?

I hope so… but probably not.

My Only Friend

The darkness is my only friend,
With no happy and bright.
I live beneath the ancient world,
And wait there for the night.

The moon and me are on good terms,
She bathes me in her glow.
Then when I see the dawn begin,
Back down beneath I go.

Over and over again,
I count each night and day.
Slowly as the years take hold,
I'll gently slip away.

Bones to rest within the dark,
Alone down there forever.
Until you come to lay there too,
So we can rest together.

The darkness is my only friend,
Though, you complete my soul.
I've waited here alone and now,
Together, we are whole.

Ink and Quill

It always will, that ink and quill,

Gracefully lick the paper.

Swirling curls and curling swirls,

This calligraphic caper.

Making letters, all the better,

A pleasant, dancing read.

To your eyes, the letters rise,

And lovingly are freed.

Lady Spring

Lord Winter the prince,

And Sir Autumn the knight,

Both sought to wed Lady Spring.

Each of them thinks,

He could claim the right,

But her heart craves the Summer King!

A.M and P.M

A.M and P.M are the very best of friends,
But can only meet together at their very ends.
For mere seconds a day do they see one another,
And spend all their time wishing more for the other.

For a whole half a day, poor A.M's heart rips,
While longing for the touch of P.M at their tips.
P.M is the same, he wants her touch too,
But for now, the seconds at their ends have to do.

They can never embrace as the time marches on,
And the seconds of touching they get are then gone.
But soon it returns, the small touch they get.
If they wait the 12 hours, they'll get to touch yet!

It kept them both happy, that second of touch.
A small but significant touch means so much!
Something to look forward to twice every day.
The feelings they have but cannot convey…

It goes on forever, unrequited, tick-tock!
Time won't stop for lovers on each phase of the clock.
Eternal, forbidden and stricken with grief.
For the seconds between, the lover's time thief!

Dear Diary

An entry for my diary,
Please keep what I write.
I'm telling you my secrets,
I hope that that's alright?

They're too heavy for my conscience.
I can't keep them on my own.
If you could share the burden,
So I'm not ever alone?

My thoughts and feelings falter,
Sometimes throughout my day.
The reason for my writing them?
My pain you keep at bay.

My happy thoughts I'd write here too,
So I would not forget.
I'm waiting for that moment,
But I haven't had one yet!

It can't be only circumstance,
It must be in my head.
Sometimes, I can't help feeling,
It might be better to be dead.

One day I might be happy,
Oh! Glory be the day!
Though now I'm always miserable,
It's always been this way.

Dear Diary, please help me!
I need help in finding ME.
I want to make it through this.
My mind needs setting free!

Dear Diary, I'm slipping!
I cannot stay here long.
All I'm ever doing,
Makes everything feel wrong!

Dear Diary, it's over!
This is where I end!
Tell them all my story,
Dear Diary, my friend…

Be You!

Our hearts, at times, are fickle.

So are, it seems, our minds.

It looks to correspond with,

The way we are designed.

Our thoughts and feelings alter,

More than seconds tick away.

We'll change the way we care and feel,

Several times a day.

Most of all we doubt,

Everything we do.

But it's better to be trying,

Than to not keep being you!

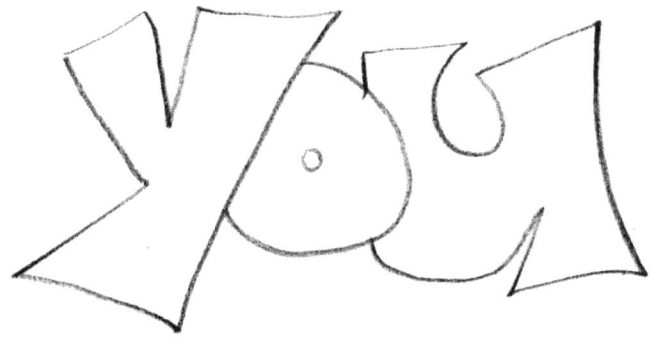

Ice Age

An ice-age is coming,
But not for the world,
For me, in my heart,
'Cause I just lost my girl.

A meteor is crashing,
But not into Earth,
Into all my feelings,
For what they are worth.

A blizzard is here,
But not one that's real,
One that reflects,
The pain that I feel.

A bushfire is raging,
But not through the trees,
Through all of my thoughts,
And it's destroying me.

A cyclone has hit,
But not at our shores,
In me deep inside,
'Cause I'm no longer yours.

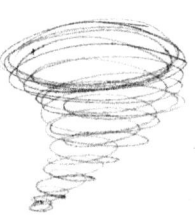

An earthquake has struck,
But not on Earth's crust,
Deep in my soul,
My whole life is crushed.

A rainbow arrives,
A real one this time,
And deep down I know,
That I will be fine.

Twice

I only have one heart to give,

And I give it all to you.

Though, if I had a second heart,

I'd give you that one too.

My third one you could have as well,

My fourth and then my fifth.

If six hearts I had to share,

Six hearts I'd love you with!

It seems though, I have only one.

I hope it will suffice.

I'll love you with my only heart,

Not only once but twice!

Poison

The poison drips upon those lips.
Death, so sweet, comes nearer.
A fatal dose, the night draws close,
And all who know her, fear her.
The final drop, the heartbeat stops,
The light drains from those eyes.
Last breath spent, abject torment,
And finally… he dies!

What if I Never?

What if I never write it,
My perfect epic ode?
What if the people can't collect,
The masterpiece they're owed?

What if they cannot read it,
My masterful quatrain?
They'll never feel the melody,
Spilling from my brain.

What if nobody hears it,
For it does not get said?
Forever jumbled nonsense,
Trapped inside my head.

What if they never know it?
For nothing would be worse.
My thoughts will not see daylight.
That sad, unwritten verse.

What if they never feel it,
The force behind my rhyme?
These lyrics without freedom,
These words lost in their prime.

I guess I better write it,
Or several of the same,
So people all around the world,
Will recognise my name!

If a Tree Should Fall

If you can't hear a tree fall in the woods,
Would you hear the whole forest fall?
Once all the trees are out of the way,
Will you remember the forest at all?

Sell all of the lumber from all of the trees,
We need all the money right now!
Don't care for the creatures or birds or bees,
They'll live somewhere else, somehow.

Once the forest is gone it'll never come back,
As long as there are people around.
The voices of people in cities are loud,
For the trees let us all make the sound!

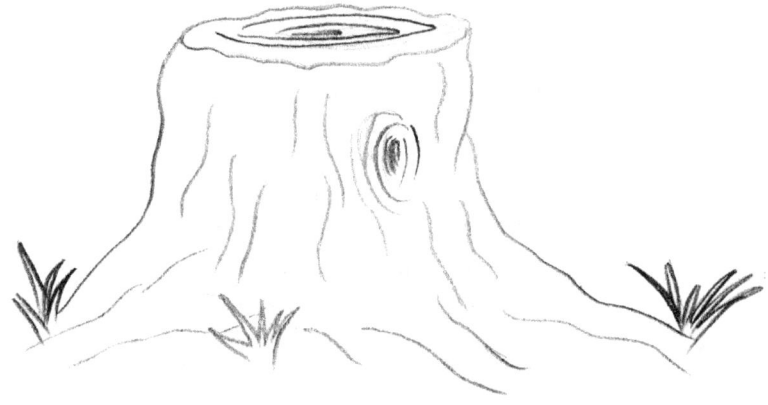

Perfect Murder

Patience is the key to it.
You'll need to bide your time.
Don't ever try it angry,
And plan the perfect crime.
Dress in balaclava,
A darker pants and shirt.
Gloves are necessary,
And always stay alert.
The night is your best cover.
The darkness is a friend.
Lurk amongst those shadows,
And clean up each loose end.
Don't let your victim bite you,
Or scratch you with their nails.
DNA offers a clue,
For detectives to unveil.
Your victim will expire,
And breathe their final breath.
No matter how you choose,
To deliver them to death.
Disposing of the body,
Is something you must brave.
You'll need to do it properly,
Avoid the shallow grave.
A fire can be helpful,
To make ash from evidence.
If you destroy all traces,
You can't be linked to an offence.
If there is a murder weapon,
Make sure it's never found.
A mineshaft or the deep blue sea,
Or deep within the ground.

Poison is an option,
That creates almost no mess.
There's no need for engaging,
And a fair chance of success.
Once you get away with it,
The feeling will return.
You must kill another.
For blood and death you yearn.
The second time is easier,
No weight upon your heart.
No fear to hold you back,
As you help someone depart.
Now you are addicted,
And killing is your sport.
You get to see your handiwork,
On every news report.
You've put fear into the populace.
All of them afraid.
Each night another murder,
An expert of your trade.
Keep doing what you're doing.
Each night your count will grow.
Never let your guard down.
No one will ever know.
Don't document your killings.
In a diary or worse,
Never put to paper,
Your crime in rhyming verse.

A Message

A message to my younger self:
Whilst times are tough for you,
Don't disappear, it's better here,
In a place beyond the blue.

Listen here, my younger self,
I've had my highs and lows.
But,
If you go, how will you know,
The life you'll yet compose?

You need to know, my younger self,
There are times it will be bad.
But,
Don't quit on me or you won't see,
The good times I have had.

A message to my younger self:
I'm you, you know, but now.
I see we battled through those times,
And made it here somehow!!

Dead Man's Moon

I've been a cattle rustler.
I've stolen all I own.
My father was a gamblin' man.
This life was in my bones.

I never knew my mother.
She died when I was young.
I grew up in saloons and bars.
The worst of every one.

I've cheated at the poker table.
I've robbed folk on the road.
I'm wanted by the sheriff.
He'll soon get what he's owed.

I killed a man out west.
I killed two more in the north.
I'm hell-bent on my survival.
I'd gladly kill a fourth.

I stole a horse on Sunday,
While folks all went to church.
They caught me on the Wednesday,
When the marshal joined the search.

I never got a trial.
The hangman on the hill.
The townsfolk came to witness.
The night was crisp and chill.

The noose around my neck now.
The light of a dead man's moon.
My anguish almost over.
I'll see my daddy soon!

My Friends

All my friends are make believe,
I'm sitting here alone.
I'm talking to myself again,
Conversing on my own.
All my friends don't argue,
Because they're me, you see?
They're far too busy agreeing,
To disagree with me.
I talk amongst my selves a lot,
Discussing everything.
From challenging to easy,
And all that's in between.
All my visions and my voices,
They never want to leave,
I won't ever be lonely,
All my friends are make believe…

Promises

He promises you the moon,
The stars and planets too.
Surely you must know,
He can't give those to you.

Something more realistic,
Would better suit his cause.
His honesty and loyalty,
Would romantically be yours.

Why start off with a lie?
If you want to have her trust,
You can't give her the moon,
The truth must be a must!

You want to impress her?
I understand the need.
But lies as a beginning,
Will likely not succeed.

Promise her your love,
All your affection too.
Promise her sincerity,
Promise her you're you!

My Demons

I have far too many reasons,
For me to be depressed.
Though, I'm loving life right now,
And can't wait to see what's next.

I hold myself together,
I keep my head up high.
Forward to the future,
A strident battle cry!

Marching on and on,
I will take on this world.
I am now unstoppable,
My sails are unfurled!

I'll fight until the end.
I'll take life on the chin.
I hear my demons knocking.
But I won't let them in!

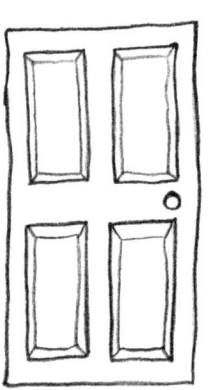

An Old Asylum

As I walk down these abandoned halls,
I hear the brick and concrete walls.
Whispered things still softly spoken,
Where fragile minds of men were broken.

Still lives the madness of time since past.
This ancient place of madmen lasts.
Each cell and room, each door and lock.
The haunting tales of walls that talk.

Shock treatment and lobotomies,
Were cutting edge technologies!
Those vicious tools, horrid devices.
Scalpels, drills and other slicers.

Still signs of blood and flesh and hair,
The scent of death that lingers there.
Tortured souls locked up to rot.
The screams and shrieks that life forgot.

In each cold cell of steel and bricks,
The raving minds of lunatics.
Lights flicker off and on again,
This place was full of fear and pain.

A place that sane minds should avoid.
Lest their reason be destroyed.
Anguish, torment, souls since lost.
Sanity comes at a cost.

I walk along and feel all this,
A lonely place, a dark abyss.
It stands here still but now lies bare.
Perhaps my walk should be elsewhere.

Grace the Stars

Now you will forever grace the stars.
We didn't get to meet you and find out who you are.
You made us both so happy for a time.
When we saw your heartbeat the feeling was sublime.

But all too fast the feeling waned.
Knowing you were gone was like a hurricane of pain.
Why did nature choose this end for you?
Hopelessness and haplessness, was there nothing we could do?

We will not forget you, we love you ever more.
Our hearts still have a special place with a tiny door,
Just for you and all you were. We always will remember.
That tiny little heartbeat on the 20th, September.

Why?

A Man: "I released all my pain through a hole in my head,
That I had put there with a small piece of lead.
My life is now over. That's how my life ends.
I've kept all my worries from family and friends."

His Wife: "I always believed I was a kind and good wife.
My husband however, chose to end his life.
His pain is now mine. It rests on my heart.
My whole life is shattered and ripped right apart!"

His Mother: "My son made his choice and ended it all.
Who knew his existence had hit such a wall?
Now the pressures of life have silenced his song.
I've failed as a parent. I've done it all wrong!"

His Brother: "My brother is dead! The bullet did well.
It's made my whole life, descend into hell.
I can't go to work. I can't eat or drink.
'What did I do wrong?' is all I can think."

His Best Mate: "Sorry mate. I didn't know. You should've spoken up.
I've known you for forever. Since we were both pups.
Life isn't that bad. I could have helped out.
I'm never the same, without you about!"

His Daughter: "Mummy just cries now since Daddy has gone.
I give her my hugs and I try to be strong.
Dad was Mum's Adam and Mummy his Eve.
If you loved us Daddy, then why did you leave?"

Albert

When I was just a boy,
I lied about my age and name,
To go and join the army,
Seeking glory, pride and fame.

I had only just turned sixteen,
But told them I was of age,
And far away to Singapore,
I went to sate my rage.

I was captured pretty early on,
Worked at gunpoint on the road,
For the Japanese in Singapore,
Much worse than I forebode.

They fed us very little,
A cup of gruel a day,
They worked us twelve hour shifts,
And our flesh melted away.

If one of us should falter,
They would shoot us then and there,
To rot upon the roadside,
Amongst the jungle air.

More than once I stumbled,
But a mate my fall would stop,
Or *my* body would be one,
Left dead out there to rot.

I missed my eighteenth birthday, And
my twenty-first as well,
All for pride and glory.
Prisoner in real-life hell.

I was one who made it back,
There were many that did not.
They say I'm one of the 'lucky ones',
But nothing I've forgot.

It sticks with me forever.
It's hell I carry round.
I relive it always,
The sights, the smells, the sounds…

The Full Moon at Midnight

The stars are numerous and shine so bright.
They light up the sky on a beautiful night.
But there's never a thing so spectacular, quite,
As the light of the full moon at midnight.

Sunset is amazing, as is the sunrise,
Or the colour reflection in a lover's eyes.
In my opinion, there's no better delight,
Than the light of the full moon at midnight.

Natural wonders, magnificent views.
Each one of nature's views you could choose.
An exceptional feeling, that shimmering light,
In those rays of the full moon at midnight.

I'd sleep through the sunshine each day if I could,
To see a full moon every evening that would,
Shine down on me, such a wonderful sight.
Perfect light of the full moon at midnight.

When my life is over and I'm at my end,
When I go to sleep forever, my friend,
Remember this and you'll be alright.
I live in the full moon at midnight.

Footprints

I followed some footprints,
Wherever they wound.
As if they were hints,
In the sand, I had found.

I followed them knowing,
Not what I would find.
My feet kept on going,
With me right behind.

I followed their journey,
As far as they stepped.
All twisting and turning,
To find where they'd crept.

I followed them closely,
To see where they end.
Curious mostly,
In which way they wend.

I followed them hoping.
My soul, it felt free.
My thoughts all eloping,
My heart full of glee.

I followed them gravely,
On down to the sea.
Then entered it bravely,
And it swallowed me…

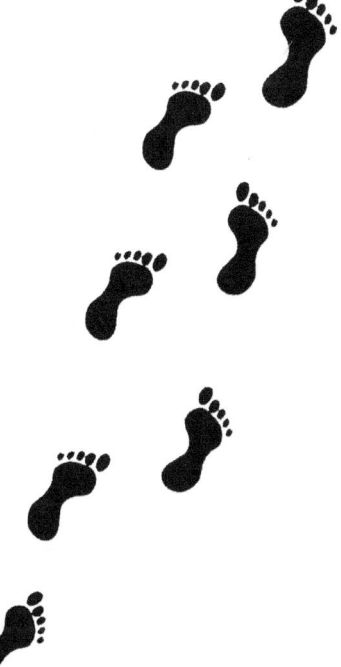

Follow

Follow the wind,
That blows in the west.
A breeze right on sunset,
Is often the best.

And follow your dreams,
Make sure they survive.
Discover your purpose,
It's why you're alive.

Follow the trail,
That winds through the trees,
Listen to nature,
The birds and the bees.

Follow the stream,
Or follow the street.
Talk to the people,
Out there you can meet.

Follow your footsteps,
Wherever they lead.
They know where to take you,
If you would take heed.

And follow your nose,
It knows where to go.
It's trying to help you,
It wants you to know.

And follow your heart,
To keep yourself free.
To stay young in spirit,
I think you'd agree.

So, follow the wind,
And follow your dreams.
Follow the trails,
The streets and the streams.
Follow your feet,
And follow your nose,
And follow your heart,
Wherever it goes…

Dancing Warmth

The flicking, licking, bounding flames,
That dance around with glee.
The clicking, cracking, sounding claims,
That call out rhythmically.

The husky, ashen flavours there,
That settle on your tongue.
In amongst the savoured air,
Surrounding everyone.

The smoky, hazy, swirling scent,
That your nose has found.
The warming, gentle, glowing heat,
That comforts those around.

Thank you for reading.

www.ingramcontent.com/pod-product-compliance
Lightning Source LLC
Chambersburg PA
CBHW072101290426
44110CB00014B/1780